Where Butterflies Fill the Sky

A Story of Immigration, Family, and Finding Home

ZAHRA MARWAN

BLOOMSBURY
CHILDREN'S BOOKS

NEW YORK LONDON OXFORD NEW DELHI SYDNEY

BLOOMSBURY CHILDREN'S BOOKS
Bloomsbury Publishing Inc., part of Bloomsbury Publishing Plc
1385 Broadway, New York, NY 10018

BLOOMSBURY, BLOOMSBURY CHILDREN'S BOOKS, and the Diana logo are trademarks of Bloomsbury Publishing Plc

First published in the United States of America in February 2022
by Bloomsbury Children's Books

Text and illustrations copyright © 2022 by Zahra Marwan

Bloomsbury books may be purchased for business or promotional use. For information on bulk purchases please contact Macmillan Corporate and Premium Sales Department at specialmarkets@macmillan.com

Library of Congress Cataloging-in-Publication Data
available upon request
ISBN 978-1-5476-0651-1 (hardcover) • ISBN 978-1-5476-0783-9 (e-book) • ISBN 978-1-5476-0784-6 (e-PDF)

Typeset in Charter
Book design by Jeanette Levy
Printed in China by Leo Paper Products, Heshan, Guangdong
2 4 6 8 10 9 7 5 3 1

To find out more about our authors and books visit www.bloomsbury.com and sign up for our newsletters.

To my parents, who should have never had to leave,
who gave us everything they could

From the desert to the sea, this is my home, where one hundred butterflies are always in the sky.

Pigeons are kept and loved.
Boats sail the calm sea.

Mama is on the shore; my aunties drink their tea.
Baba swims in the open water.

His sister
takes the boat
out to sea.

Me and my brothers are in our own world.

This is where I sleep,
where my ancestors live and
are always watching.

My aunties hold me close.

They try to protect me the only way they know how.

People say we don't belong here.

We have to leave our home.

Baba tells me there is magic
in the place we'll go.

I don't want to leave. Mama says it will be better for us.

I say my goodbyes without knowing why

and travel far, far away

. . . to a new place where each day feels like a year.

Where no one speaks like me.

Are my ancestors still watching?

Baba walks in the river and Mama sits under the cottonwood tree.

My brothers are in
their own world.

We hear a noise and follow it.
It's the music of a guitarrón.

People dance. They are happy.

And when we look up . . .

one hundred balloons fill the sky.

I'm so different from everyone here.

But these new people show me I belong.

My family sends reminders that they are thinking of me,

and I tell them that I'm thinking of them, too. That I miss them, and hope we can be together again.

That in this new place of high desert, I have found a home.

THE STORY OF MY FAMILY

I was born in Kuwait in 1989 to a Kuwaiti mother and stateless father. My father was Kuwaiti in speech, dress, and culture. Just like my mom, he was born in Sharq, in 1948 in a neighborhood primarily made up of old Iranian families. Kuwait was under British control (by mutual agreement) between 1899 and 1961, and when it formally became an independent country, its government attempted to register everyone who met the requirements of citizenship.

The concept of official citizenship was foreign to many people. Bedouin tribes had freely wandered the land for generations, and people weren't used to this level of government involvement. Some of the requirements for citizenship were unclear. For some families, including my father's, illiteracy (the inability to read and write) meant that the message just didn't reach them. By the time his family learned that they should have registered, it was too late. And since Kuwaiti law says that citizenship is passed down through the father's side, this means my brothers and I were born stateless, too.

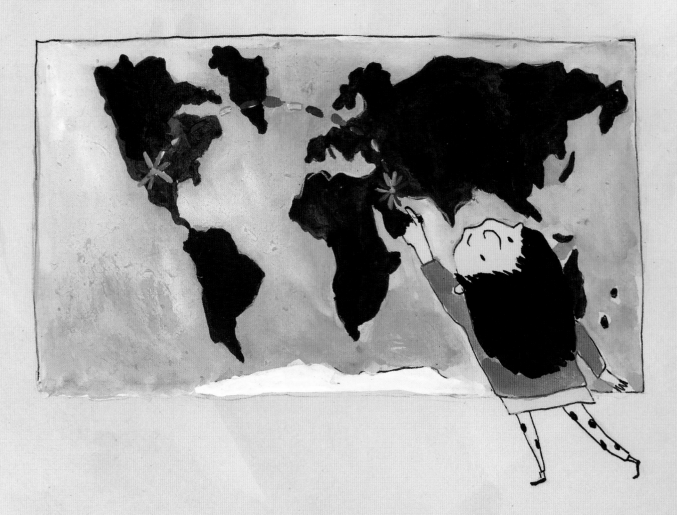

Life for my father as a stateless man in the 1950s to 1970s was similar and almost equal to the life of a Kuwaiti citizen, but as Iraqis fled Saddam Hussein's rule in the 1980s and attempted to settle in our country as stateless residents themselves, discriminatory laws began to be established. Before long, stateless people were considered illegal residents. They weren't allowed to attend public school or go to college. They couldn't access health care. They couldn't get married, and they couldn't leave the country, because they weren't sure if they would be allowed back. Their only career options were working low-wage jobs or joining the army.

There also wasn't a clear path for most stateless residents to become official citizens. My parents saw no future for me and my brothers in the only home they and we had ever known. After my father fought his whole life to be recognized in his country, even losing a brother who served in the Kuwait army during the invasion by Iraq, my parents immigrated to New Mexico with broken hearts—but also the hope of securing us our basic human rights and the ability to pursue happy lives.

As a young child in New Mexico's public schools, I was taught to be proud of my heritage—maybe because so many of my neighbors had strong Indigenous and Hispano roots and had been subject to so much cultural oppression themselves. I lost the ability to live among my family, language, and culture because of government rules, but I carry with me a constant sense of home.

My heart goes out to the nearly 100,000 stateless people still in Kuwait, some of them my family.

ABOUT THE ART

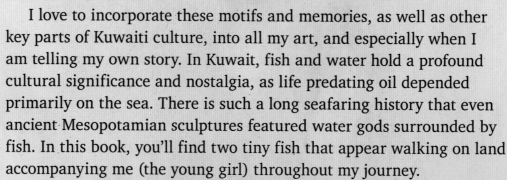

So much of my memory of childhood feels dreamlike. A collage
of different people, places, and things that all appear at once.
I remember the comfort of living in a place that my parents
and grandparents were from. Where everyone dresses
similarly, speaks the same, and has familiar cultural
habits. I remember pale greens and yellows from the
humidity and desert climate. The sea was sometimes
turquoise, sometimes dark blue, and so often warm.

There are so many particularities of both places
that I call home that make them feel magical in real life.
Loving and caring for birds, the uniformity of dressing in
black, the way family holds a key place in Kuwaiti life and society,
and the warmth and generosity of heart. The music and blue sky in
New Mexico, the kind hearts of the people. It's magical to see the hot-air
balloons every day in the fall. Mysticism abounds in both cultures, like the bukhoor, or
Arabic myrrh, that we use for protection in Kuwait. The scent is so beautiful and strong,
and we believe it can ward off evil.

I love to incorporate these motifs and memories, as well as other
key parts of Kuwaiti culture, into all my art, and especially when I
am telling my own story. In Kuwait, fish and water hold a profound
cultural significance and nostalgia, as life predating oil depended
primarily on the sea. There is such a long seafaring history that even
ancient Mesopotamian sculptures featured water gods surrounded by
fish. In this book, you'll find two tiny fish that appear walking on land
accompanying me (the young girl) throughout my journey.

There is also a culture of keeping birds, from pigeons to falcons,
especially on the rooftops of the Gulf. There's a parrot in the book that
really lives with my aunt. He hangs upside down and says "meow." The
boys with the pigeons on the first page are Razi and Reza. Their mother
would babysit my oldest brother when he was very young, while my mom went to work.
The boys would visit with their pet pigeon each day. Tragically, on a trip to visit family in
Iran with their mom, the boys' passenger ship sank in the gulf. The ship with balloons I
drew is my hope that their spirits found peace.

There are two bulls that I refer to as my ancestors (a serious cultural faux pas, but one that is meaningful to me). They're based off art from the ancient Dilmun civilization found in Kuwait and Failaka Island among ancient Greek ruins. I was happy to be able to see these in person during my last two visits home, both on Failaka Island and in the antiquities museum of Dar al-Athar al-Islamiyyah, a former American hospital where my aunt was born in the 1960s and which now houses art. You can find them in the story watching over me as I sleep.

There really are hundreds of butterflies in the Kuwaiti sky, especially when spring migration brings scores of painted ladies to the country. There also really are hundreds of hot-air balloons in Albuquerque's October sky, during the International Balloon Fiesta. And each year, my friend plays his guitarrón while taking a ninety-mile walk to Chimayó so he can feel close to his ancestors.

I created these paintings traditionally. First by sketching, then by refining my lines and adding ink and watercolor washes. The book's palette, including the paper I chose, comes from the way both places feel. Bright and sunny with saturated colors, old buildings in Kuwait made of mud and materials from the sea, those in New Mexico from traditional adobe bricks. I hope that you can feel the beauty of these two places I love through the illustrations I've shared.